This book is dedicated to my sisters:

IRENE, RUTH, and NETTIE.

JETS AND ROCKETS

and How They Work

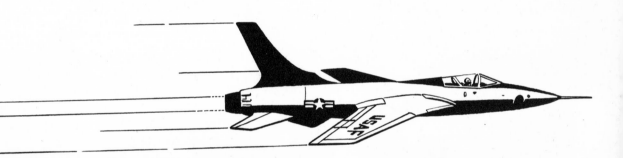

JETS AND ROCKETS
and How They Work

by WILLIAM P. GOTTLIEB

Photographs by the author. Drawings by John W. Marshall, Paul Hodge, and Ed Dahlin. Foreword by William J. O'Donnell

GARDEN CITY BOOKS
Garden City, New York

Contents

10 – 9 – 8 – 7 – 6 –

Library of Congress Catalog Card Number 59-8611 Copyright © 1959 by William P. Gottlieb. Adapted from the filmstrip, "Flying with Jets and Rockets," from the set, "Science Facts About Transportation," published by the Text-Film Department of the McGraw-Hill Book Company, and produced by the William P. Gottlieb Company, New York City. Illustration of Republic F-105 "Thunderchief" on page 2 courtesy of American Modeler. Illustration of North American X-15 on page 53 courtesy of Reaction Motors. Printed in the United States of America.

Foreword

Today, jet planes can streak through the sky at thousands of miles an hour. And not too many years from now, rockets will probably carry men to the moon and beyond. How do these remarkable jet and rocket machines work?

The achievements of jets and rockets are due mostly to their distinctive methods of propulsion. The purpose of this book, therefore, is to explain the scientific principles which drive the engines of these amazing ships. There will be little said about engineering details, for these change from year to year. Instead, you will learn about ideas which have been known for a long time, and which will continue to be the basis of jet and rocket propulsion in the future.

This broad approach, together with the book's unique step-by-step illustrations and "at home" experiments, should help you gain a more accurate understanding of our modern mechanical age.

WILLIAM J. O'DONNELL
Chief Engineer, Research and Development
Republic Aviation Corporation

4 – 3 – 2 – 1 – ZERO !

Air Is Real

To understand how jets and rockets work, you must first know something about air; and the most important thing to know is that air is real.

6

Air may seem like "nothing"; yet you can feel it as it blows across your face and through your hair . . . or makes a kite tug against its line. . . .

You can hear air, too, as it sings through a trumpet or whistles through a window crack. . . .

And, while you can't actually see air, you can see what it does as it bends tall grass, or sends seeds floating, or pushes a sailboat across the water.

What *is* air?

Air is a gas. Actually, it is a mixture of several gases, mostly nitrogen and oxygen.

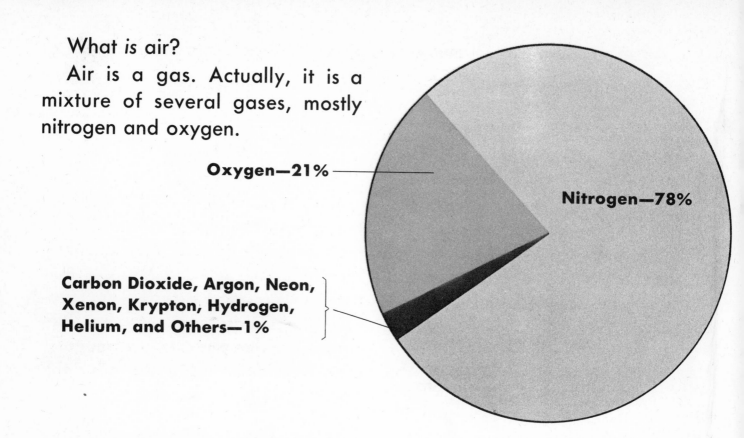

Oxygen—21%

Nitrogen—78%

Carbon Dioxide, Argon, Neon, Xenon, Krypton, Hydrogen, Helium, and Others—1%

Like all substances, gas is made up of extremely small particles, called molecules. It is these molecules which, when the wind blows, bump into the sails of a sailboat and push it along.

No Wind

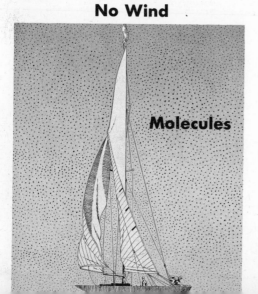

Molecules

(In the drawings in this book, molecules are sometimes shown as dots you can "see." Remember, however, that actual molecules are so tiny that you can't see them, and so closely packed that there can be millions in a cubic inch.)

Wind

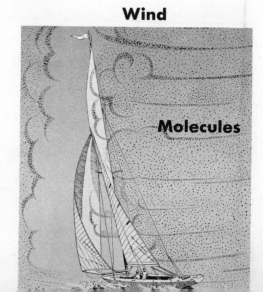

Molecules

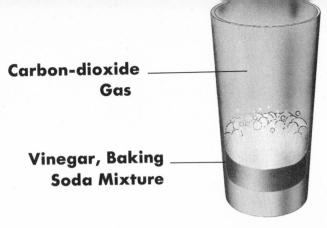

Carbon-dioxide Gas

Vinegar, Baking Soda Mixture

Here's a simple way to see that gas is real, even though it may be invisible:

Put a half teaspoonful of baking soda (bicarbonate of soda) into a large glass. Add a teaspoonful of vinegar.

These two "chemicals," when mixed, produce a heavy gas called carbon dioxide, which swells and fills the glass. Because carbon-dioxide molecules are heavier than air, they remain in the glass. For proof that they're there, and very real . . . carefully tilt the glass, so that the invisible carbon dioxide pours into a trough of aluminum foil and flows onto the flame of a lighted candle.

Presto! The invisible gas molecules smother the flame!

Incidentally, carbon dioxide is the gas used in many fire extinguishers.

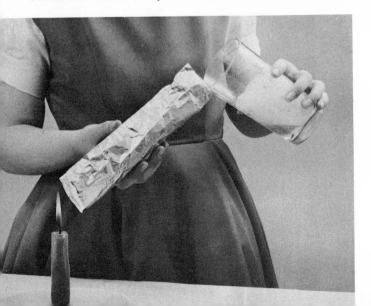

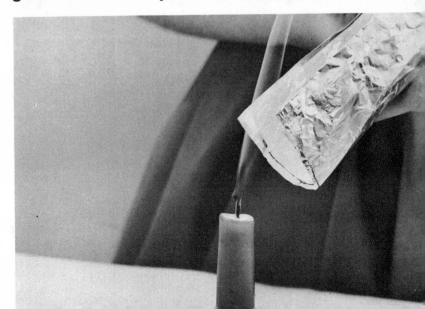

Air Can Push

Many people think a jet plane moves forward because gas shooting out from the nozzle pushes against something.

This is not true.

A jet's movement comes from the push of molecules against the *front* of its engine. Because this is one of the most important scientific principles you can learn about jets (and rockets, too), let's study the matter carefully.

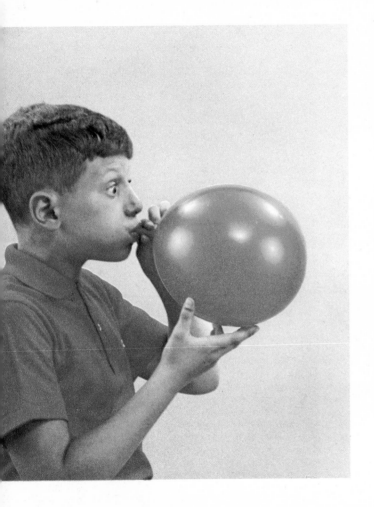

A toy balloon can help demonstrate how the force of air molecules can move a jet plane.

First, blow up a balloon until it is full of air. Hold the end tightly. Then suddenly let go and . . .

whoosh! As air shoots out from the nozzle, the balloon spurts away.
Where does the power come from? What determines the direction of its flight?

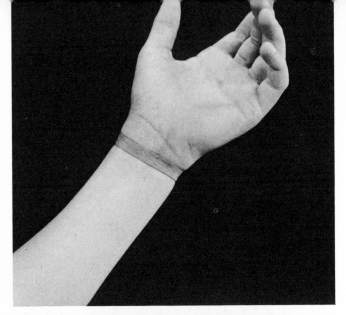
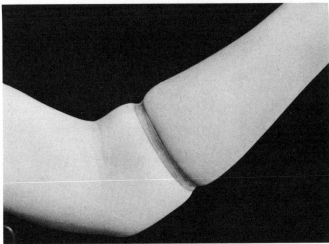
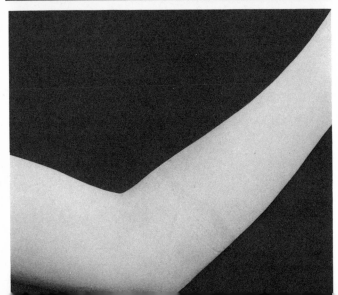

Before learning what happened to the balloon, first try this experiment:

Get a rubber band that just about fits your wrist without stretching.

Next, move the rubber band higher up on your arm. The rubber stretches and the band becomes bigger. But it doesn't get as big around as your arm normally is, because the rubber molecules are "elastic" . . . they want to return to their original size. So they squeeze inward until they pack the molecules in your arm tightly together.

The elastic rubber can squeeze just so far and no farther, because the molecules in your arm are elastic, too. *They* want to return to *their* original size. So they, in turn, push outward against the rubber band, as much as the rubber will let them. If you remove the rubber band, this outward force will pop your arm right back into place.

There is, as you can see, a kind of struggle between the molecules in the rubber band and those in your arm.

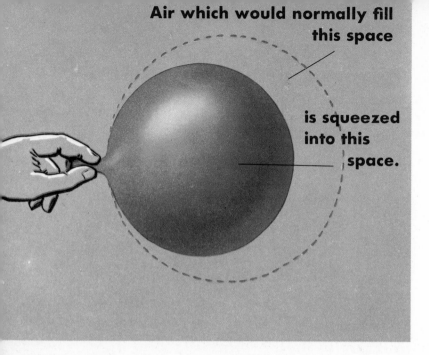

Air which would normally fill this space

is squeezed into this space.

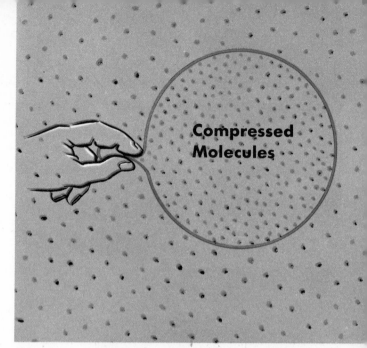

Compressed Molecules

The same sort of struggle takes place between the molecules of a rubber balloon and the air molecules inside the balloon.

When you fill a balloon, you blow a large mass of air into it. But the elastic walls try to return to normal size. They squeeze the air molecules closely together, into a smaller space, until they can squeeze no farther.

Air is elastic, too; and its compressed molecules try to return to the less crowded space *they* normally fill. So they push outward against the balloon walls, as much as they can. The harder the balloon squeezes, the harder the air pushes back.

14

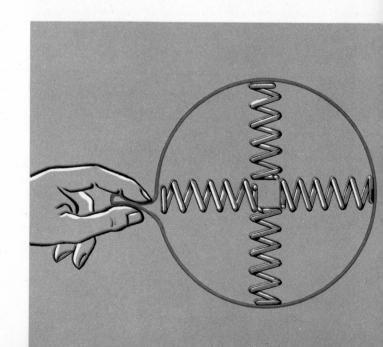

The force of billions of air molecules, pressing against the balloon walls, is as powerful as the push of steel springs. There is enough force in this "air pressure" to send the balloon flying. However . . .

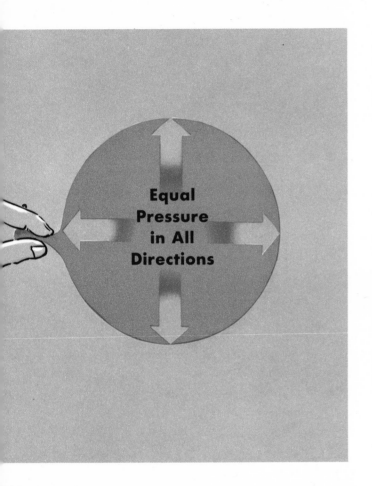

Equal
Pressure
in All
Directions

the molecules are pressing equally in all directions. No matter how hard the molecules push *one* way, other molecules push equally hard the *opposite* way.

Because the forces inside a closed balloon are in perfect balance, they are "tied up" and cannot act.

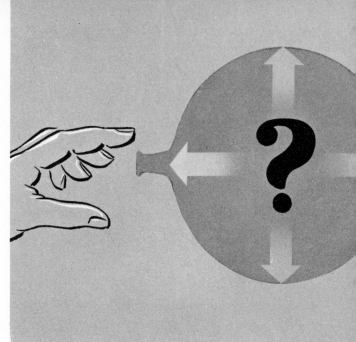

No, this closed balloon will not fly.

However, by opening the nozzle, you can "untie" the forces inside and send the balloon spurting through the air.

Although an open balloon swoops this way and that, it doesn't go off in just *any* direction. Despite its turns and twists, it moves more or less away from its nozzle. Why?

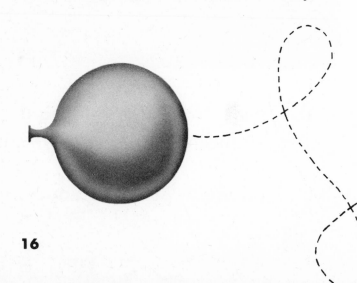

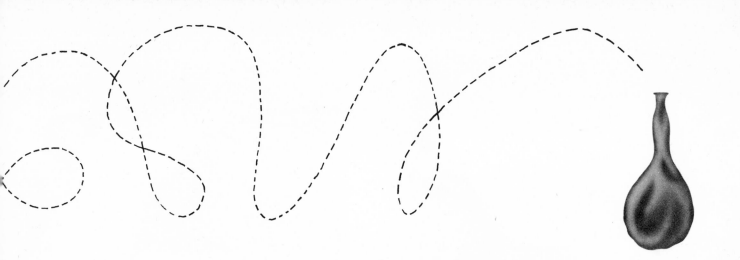

The balloon won't move sideways to the nozzle because the pressure on any side wall is balanced by the pressure on the opposite side wall (see below—left).

But the pressure on the front wall is greater than the pressure against the wall which contains the nozzle (see below—right). That's because molecules are escaping through the nozzle instead of pushing.

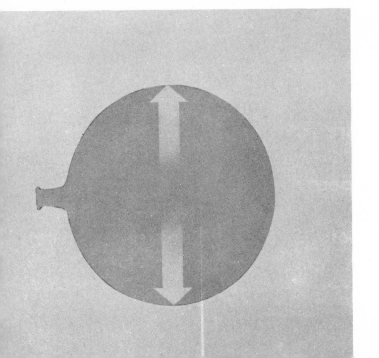

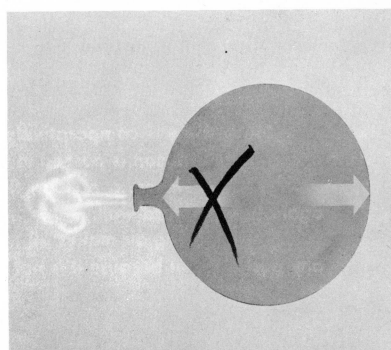

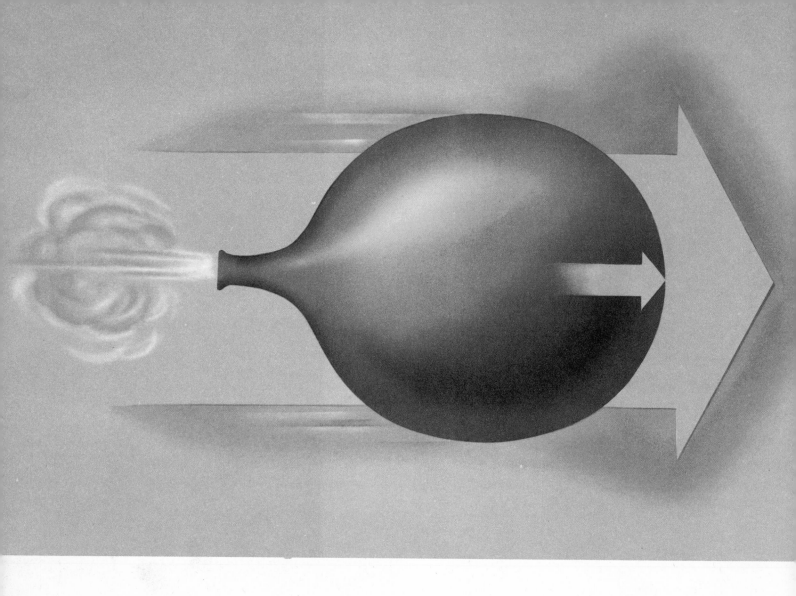

Since there is comparatively more force on the wall opposite the opening, the balloon is pushed in that direction.

In other words, a balloon flies because of the push of molecules against the forward wall.

The escaping air makes all this possible . . . not because it is doing any pushing, but because it is *not* doing any pushing.

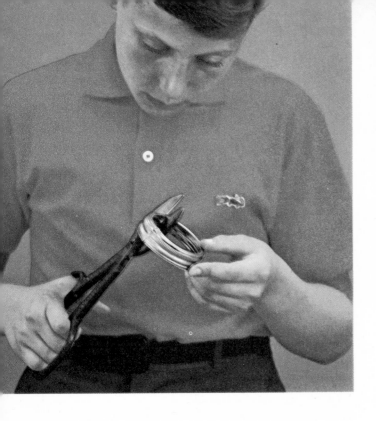

Here's an experiment which should demonstrate these ideas clearly.

First, get the ring from a mason-jar cap. Cut off about one third of the ring with a tin shears.

Replace the missing part of the ring with a piece of paper, as shown above.

Next, get a basketball or other large ball. Put something under it, so it won't roll. Then place the ring on top of the ball and fill it with marbles.

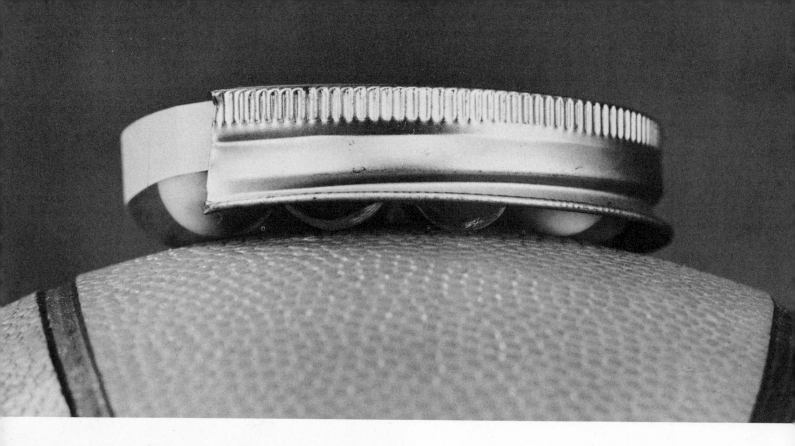

Be sure to place the outer marbles under the lip of the ring so that the entire ring is raised off the basketball and is resting, instead, on the marbles. That way, the ring can roll easily in any direction.

But the ring *won't* roll.

Because of gravity, each marble "tries" to go down its own side of the basketball. This makes the marbles press against the inside of the ring.

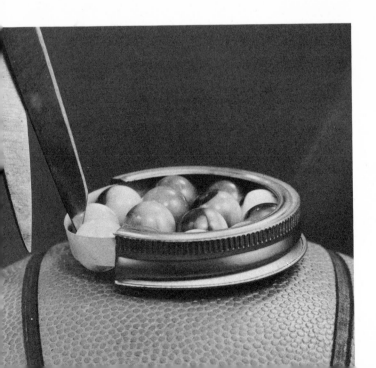

Since the marbles press equally against *all* sides of the closed ring, the ring doesn't move. It stays balanced on the basketball.

But now, open one end of the ring by *carefully* cutting the paper with a pair of sharp scissors. Naturally, the marbles near the open end will roll out. And, since there will then be less force on *that* side . . .

21

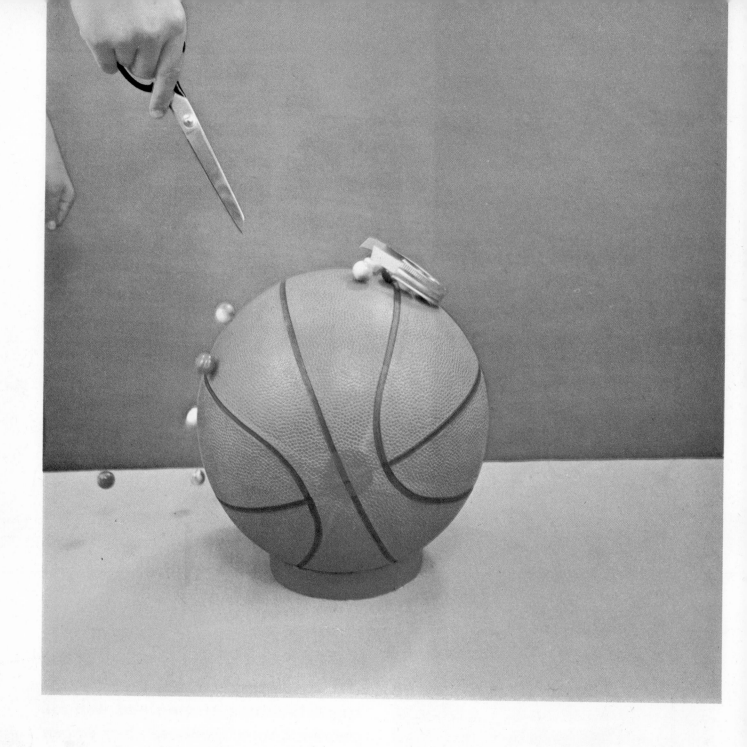

... the ring will suddenly roll away in the direction *opposite* from the opening.

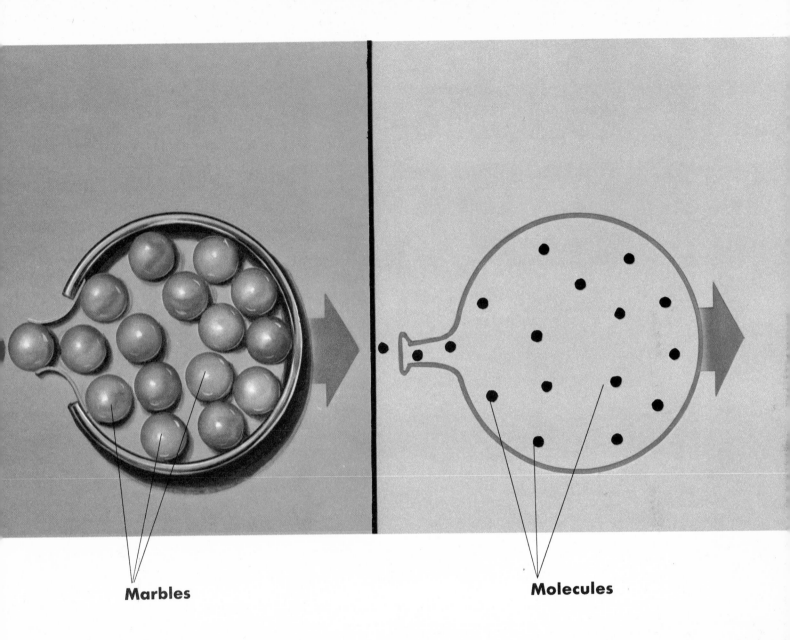

Marbles

Molecules

Whether it's a ring with marbles or a balloon with molecules, the object moves away from its open end be-cause the force on the closed end is greater, and not because of any push from the open end.

From a Painting by Sir Godfrey Kneller

Action and Reaction

About 250 years ago, Sir Isaac Newton, the great English scientist, discovered several laws of motion. One of them said this: *to every action, there is an equal and opposite reaction.* Or, to say it even more simply: whatever pushes gets pushed back equally.

Everything from bikes to battleships is driven according to the law of action and reaction. But jets, rockets, and rubber balloons make such clear and direct use of this principle that they, in particular, are often known as "reaction engines."

Here's a way to demonstrate that to every action, there's a reaction:

Place a block of wood next to the six-inch mark of a ruler (1).

Then shoot a marble against it (2).

The wood will move one way; and the marble, the other (3).

It's obvious why the wood moved. It was pushed by the marble. But why did the *marble* rebound? Because the wood "resisted" and, in effect, pushed back against the marble.

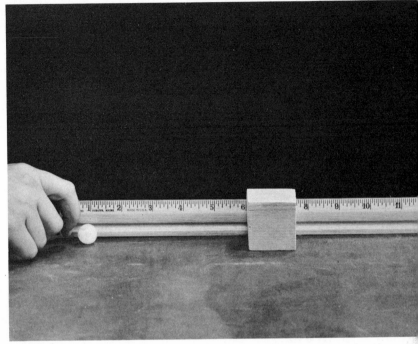

(1)

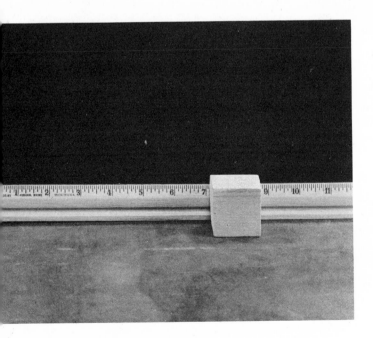

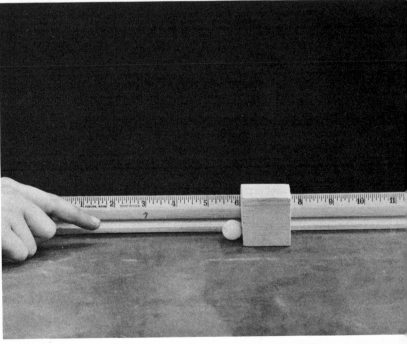

(2)

To see more clearly how an action produces an opposite and equal reaction, squeeze two balloons together. Push with only one balloon. Keep the other steady.

The "pusher" balloon is compressed by the force of the push. But, as you can see, the other balloon is compressed just as much. It pushes back, and with equal force. (In fact, it is impossible to tell which balloon is "acting" and which is "reacting.")

As further proof that the action and reaction are opposite and equal, let go suddenly. The compressed balloons will spring back into shape and push each other equally far in opposite directions.

Though only a "microscope" eye could have seen it, the same thing happened with the marble and the block of wood. Their surfaces squeezed against each other with opposite and equal force. The marble rebounded farther than the wood, but only because it was lighter and because it could roll.

Now let's return to our flying balloon and see how the law of action and reaction applies to it.

A mass of compressed air molecules presses against the front wall of the open balloon and pushes it forward. That's the *action*. The wall pushes back against the air molecules and sends them out the nozzle. That's the *reaction*. (Sometimes you'll see it stated the opposite way: the escaping molecules are called the "action" and the moving balloon is called the "reaction." As you saw when you squeezed two balloons together, it's practically impossible to distinguish between the thing that's acting and the thing that's reacting . . . and perhaps it doesn't really matter.)

Here's another way to see how a mass of molecules can push an object and, in turn, be thrown back:

Stand on the back of a rowboat. With your body (which is a mass of molecules), push against the boat. Your push will send the boat across the water. Simultaneously, the boat will push back against you and send you flying into the water.

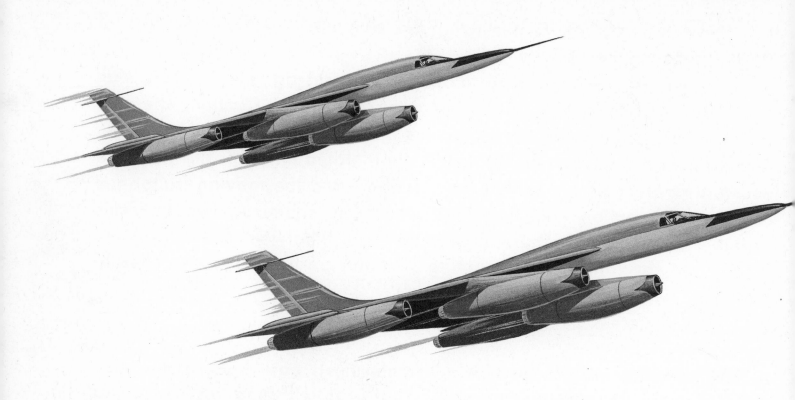

How Jet Engines Develop Thrust

Though a jet plane usually weighs more than several automobile trucks and may speed along at more than a thousand miles an hour, it nonetheless gets its push (or "thrust") from air molecules, just as our balloon did.

How can something as light as air push hard enough against an engine wall to make a giant plane fly . . . and fly fast?

You've already seen that if a large mass of air is compressed, it can push a balloon. You also must know that air, if it blows fast, can knock over trees. So . . .

If an engine can compress a large enough mass of air . . . And if it can make the air move fast enough . . .

Then it can create the thrust to fly a plane.

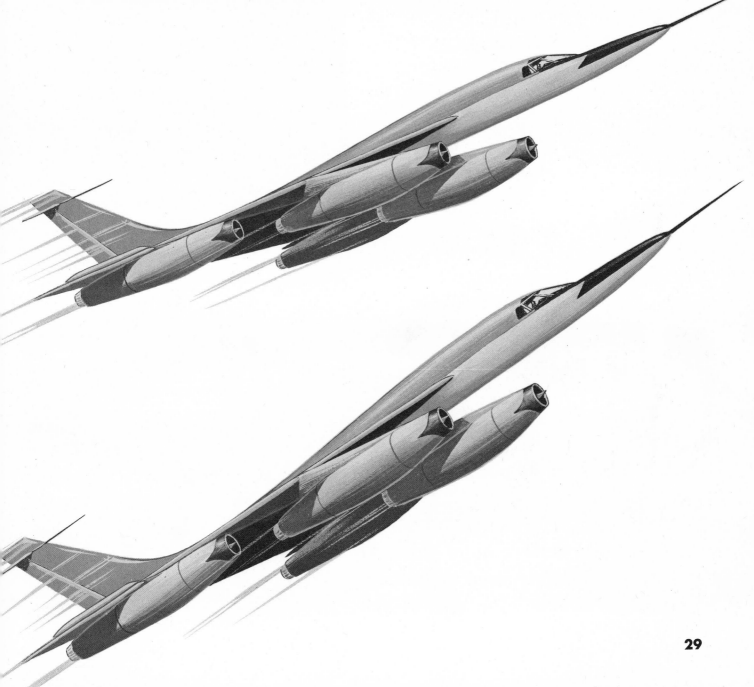

To pull in enough air and to make the air move fast, a jet engine uses these principal parts:

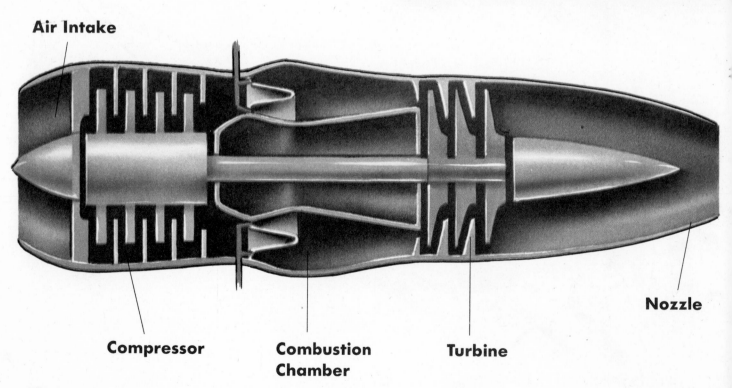

Air Intake

Compressor

Combustion Chamber

Turbine

Nozzle

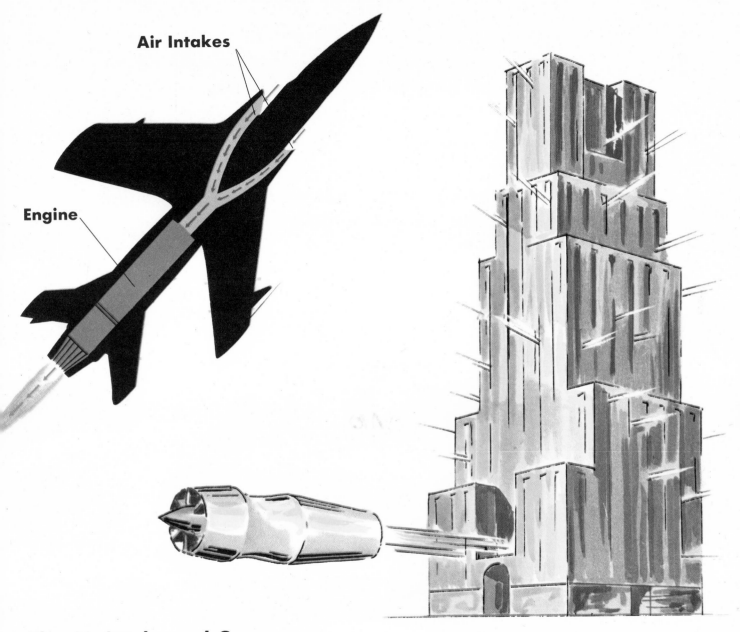

Air Intakes

Engine

The Air Intake and Compressor

As you might expect, a huge mass of air is required to push a jet. In fact, a single engine uses enough in a few minutes to fill a large office building.

This air comes in through an intake at the front end of the engine. When a plane streaks through the sky at several hundred miles an hour, its intake, by itself, might be able to scoop up all the air that was needed and ram it tightly into the engine. But at slower speeds, and especially when the plane starts and takes off, the intake must be aided by a "compressor."

A compressor is an air pump made up of rows of whirling blades, like several rows of electric fans all on the same shaft.

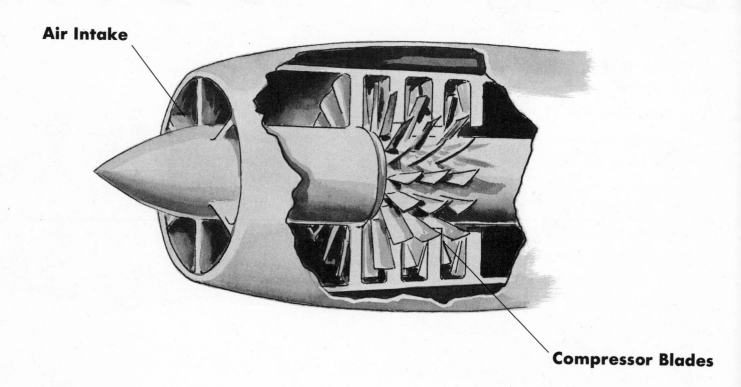

Air Intake

Compressor Blades

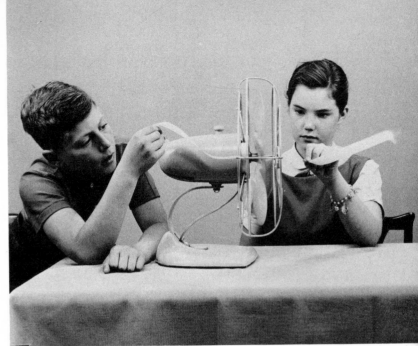

To see what compressor blades do, carefully hold one limp ribbon in back of a fan, another in front.

Then turn on the motor.

The ribbon on one side will be sucked in toward the fan. The other ribbon will be blown away. In other words, the fan pulls in air from one end, then pushes it to the other.

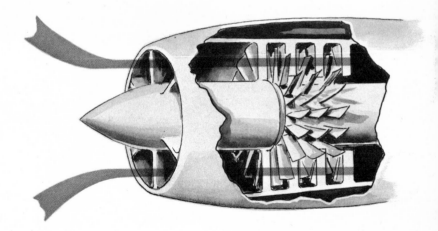

That's how the compressor of a jet engine works, too. It pulls in the outside air and pushes it into the combustion chamber.

The Combustion Chamber

A compressor rams tightly packed air molecules into the combustion chamber. As in a rubber balloon, the compressed molecules push with great pressure. To increase their power, the molecules are speeded up. This is done by heating them with burning fuel, such as kerosene.

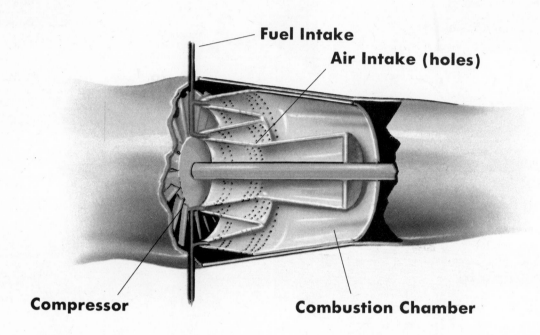

Fuel Intake

Air Intake (holes)

Compressor

Combustion Chamber

When most things are heated, they expand. That's because molecules, which are *always* moving and bumping into each other, move more vigorously when the temperature rises and therefore bounce each other farther apart.

To see what happens when air is heated, do this: snap a balloon on an empty bottle and place the bottle in a pan of water on a hot stove. The heat

will make the air molecules in the bottle move vigorously and bounce further apart. As the air expands, it pushes against the bottle. But the bot-

tle can't stretch to hold this "extra air." Instead, the extra volume of air pushes out of the open end of the bottle and soon fills the balloon.

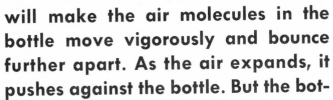

Heated Air

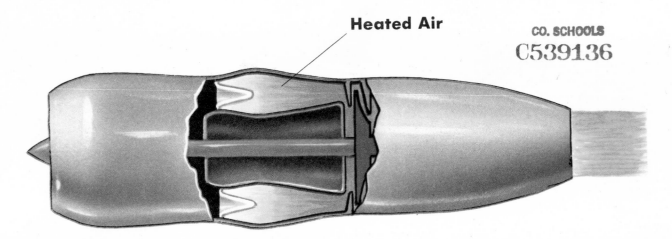

In a jet, the same thing happens. Burning fuel in the combustion chamber heats the compressed air and expands it greatly. The extra air has no place to go but out. So out it rushes towards the large open nozzle, just as fast as it can go.

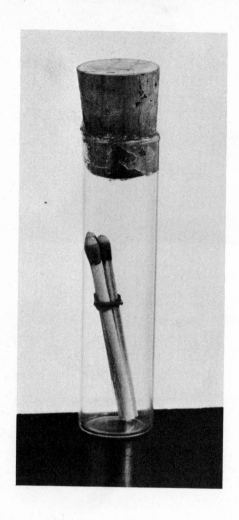

For an idea of the force of heated air, try an experiment which uses direct combustion.

For fuel, use two or three wooden matches. With a rubber band, tie their heads together and drop them in a glass pill-bottle. Cork the bottle, after first smearing vaseline where the cork and bottle touch. (The vaseline will help give you an airtight seal. It will also keep the cork from sticking.)

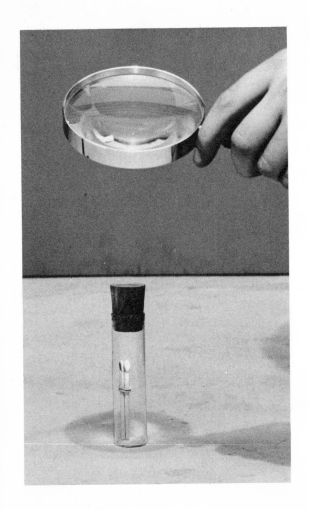

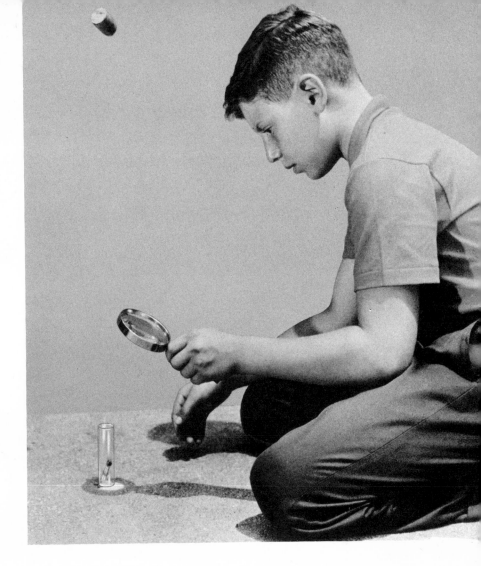

Now, you're ready for the next step. Take the bottle outside into the sunlight. With a magnifying glass, focus the sun's rays on the match heads. Soon, the matches will catch fire. Then, in a split second . . .

Pop goes the cork!

It was pushed out by the increasing pressure of the expanding gas. (Let's start using the word "gas" instead of "air"; because now fuel molecules have been added to the air molecules.)

The Turbine

In a jet engine, the heated, fast-moving gas strikes the blades of a turbine and spins it.

The purpose of the turbine is to drive the compressor, to which it is attached by a shaft. When the turbine is spun by hot, racing gas, the compressor turns with it.

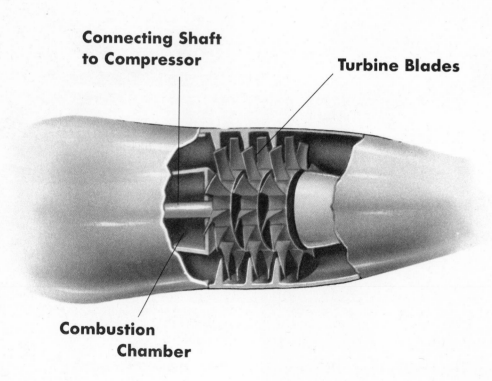

**Connecting Shaft
to Compressor**

Turbine Blades

**Combustion
Chamber**

Here's a way to see how hot gas can turn a turbine:

Put some water in a clean oil can of the type shown, or in any other metal container with a tiny opening. (An ordinary teakettle isn't satisfactory, because its spout is too big; but a "singing kettle" will do.)

Next, heat the can of water until a jet of steam (a gas) spurts out. *BUT BE CAREFUL.* KEEP YOUR HANDS AND FACE AWAY FROM THE JET. IT IS VERY HOT.

Now place a pinwheel in the jet stream. The escaping hot gas, with its force concentrated by a tiny spout, has enough power to spin the pinwheel round and round.

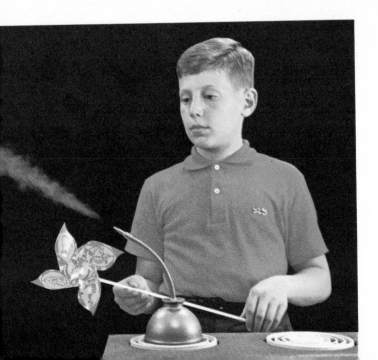

Incidentally, the "steam turbine" principle is used not only for turning jet-plane compressors, but other types of machinery too, including the propellers of ocean liners and atomic submarines.

In the last picture on page 39, you can see how the force of the steam seems to be scattered and weakened by the time it gets through the pin wheel. In a jet engine, too, most of the force of the gas is used up when it hits and turns the turbine blades.

The Nozzle

However, the gas in the nozzle, though less compressed and cooler than in the middle of the engine, still has enough mass and speed to produce a great deal of force. And it is this force—the amount left in the nozzle—that gives thrust to the plane.

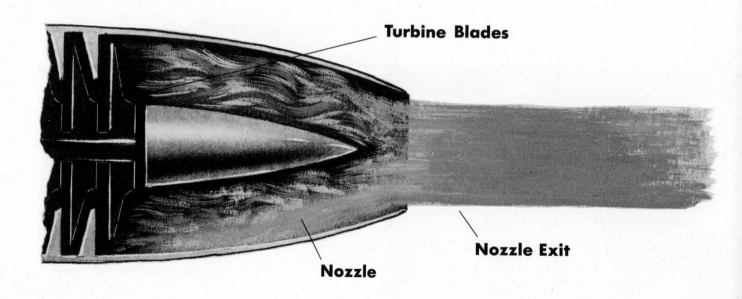

Turbine Blades

Nozzle

Nozzle Exit

As in a rubber balloon, the pressure inside the nozzle pushes out in all directions. And, since there's a nozzle exit, there is no force against that side; and the jet spurts forward.

You may wonder why gas doesn't escape out the front end of the engine, through the same opening that lets the gas in.

The explanation is this: the incoming air moves under such pressure that it acts almost like a solid wall. Therefore, the expanding gases take the easier way out . . . through the nozzle.

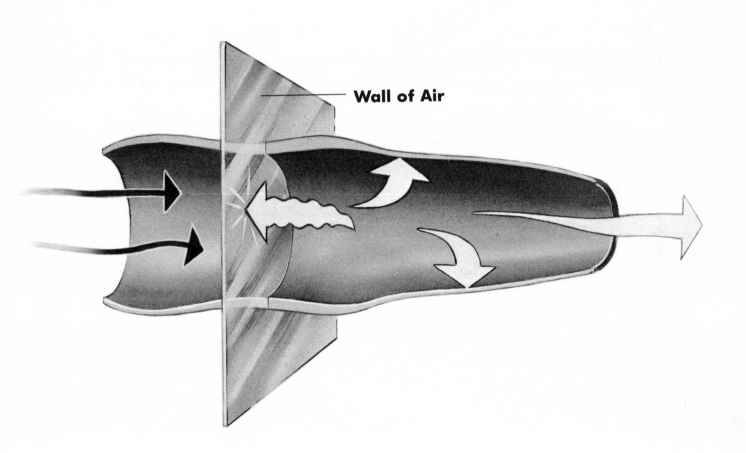

Wall of Air

Three Kinds of Jet Engines

It may be hard to believe that the same air we breathe can make a gigantic plane like this roar through the sky. But you've seen that it can . . . and faster than ordinary plane engines with propellers.

(Jets are smoother, too, for they work with one continuous swoosh! Ordinary engines have many separate cylinder explosions.)

42

There are several kinds of jet engines. The most widely used is the turbojet, which is the kind you've just been reading about. The turbojet gets its name from its turbine.

Here is a brief review of how a turbojet works. Large masses of air are pulled in through the intake and then compressed. The compressed air is heated and expanded in a combustion chamber. The expanded air rushes against a turbine and spins it. The spinning turbine turns the compressor and keeps fresh air coming in. The old air, reaching the nozzle, is compressed enough and is moving fast enough to provide pressure to push the plane. And because there is a nozzle exit in the rear, the force against the front sends the plane shooting forward.

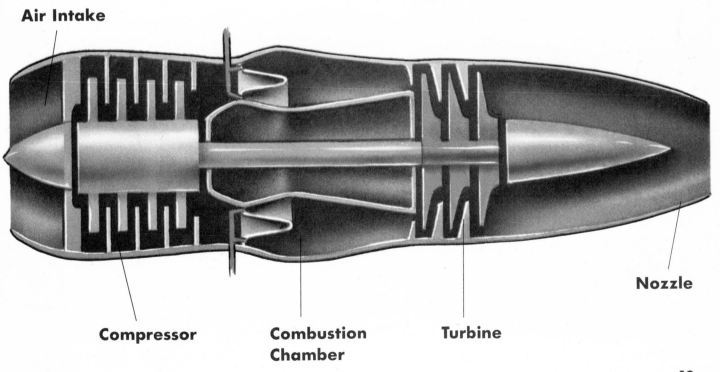

Air Intake

Compressor

Combustion Chamber

Turbine

Nozzle

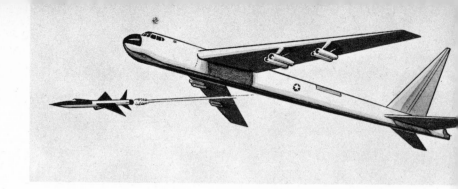

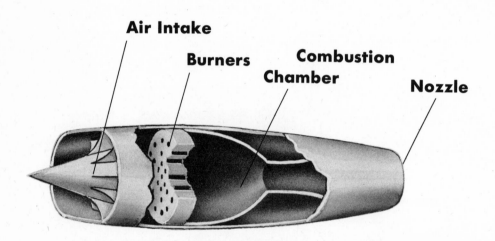

Air Intake

Burners

Combustion Chamber

Nozzle

Another type of jet is the ram-jet. Instead of using a compressor, it depends on its own forward speed to scoop up air and ram it into the combustion chamber. Here, the compressed air is heated and expanded to increase pressure. A large nozzle in the rear creates a pressure imbalance and gives thrust to the forward end of the engine.

Since the ram-jet needs no compressor, it therefore needs no turbine or any other moving parts.

The trouble with a ram-jet is that, in order to scoop up enough air, it must be flying at least a few hundred miles an hour. To reach that speed, it has to be carried aloft by another plane or shot into the air with rockets.

44

A third type of jet engine is the turboprop. With this type, there are two turbines. One turbine spins the compressor. Another spins a conventional propeller. In other words, this engine uses both a propeller and the direct force of gases.

The turboprop isn't as fast as other jets; but it uses fuel more economically. And it is both faster and smoother running than ordinary propeller-driven craft.

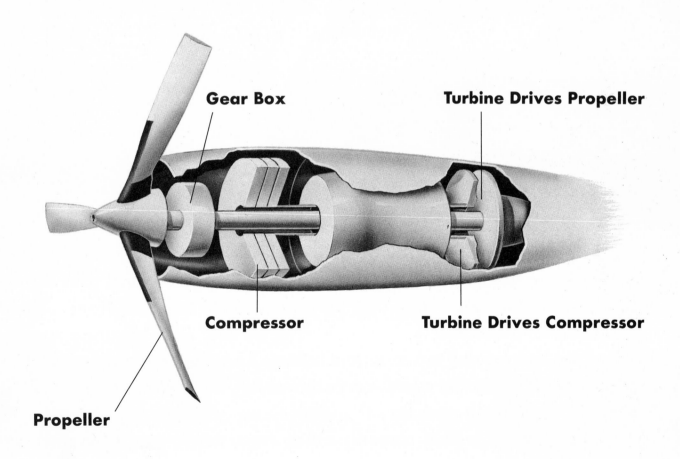

Gear Box **Turbine Drives Propeller**

Compressor **Turbine Drives Compressor**

Propeller

Earth's Atmosphere

Will Jets Get to the Moon?

Jets are marvelous machines. They can fly at great speeds and at great heights. But they will never be able to take us to the moon and beyond. Jets need masses of compressed and heated air to develop pressure. Also, for their fuel to burn, they need oxygen, which comes from the air.

But in outer space, there is *no* air.

 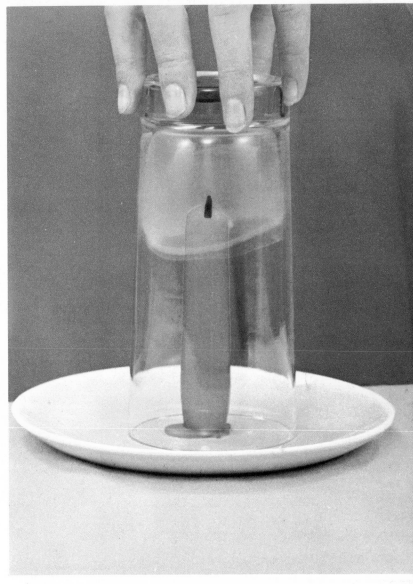

To see what would happen to burning fuel in outer space, place a candle on a plate. Then light the candle. It burns just as long as it can use the oxygen in the air.

Next, cover the lit candle with a glass. Soon the flame will use up all the oxygen in the glass. Since oxygen from outside the glass cannot get inside, the flame will starve and die.

How Rockets Work

Jets won't work in outer space. But rockets will, because they don't need air.

Rockets do need oxygen; but they carry their own supply, either in solid or liquid form.

48

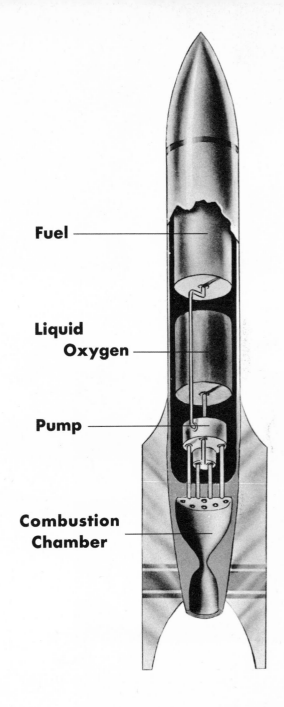

Fuel

Liquid Oxygen

Pump

Combustion Chamber

If it is difficult for you to imagine a gas in some different form, think of the fact that steam (a gas) comes from water (a liquid), which in turn can become ice (a solid). All three are the same substance, at different temperatures.

Like steam, oxygen can be turned into either liquid or solid form.

In a liquid-fuel rocket, tanks of liquid fuel and liquid oxygen are pumped into the combustion chamber, where they are ignited.

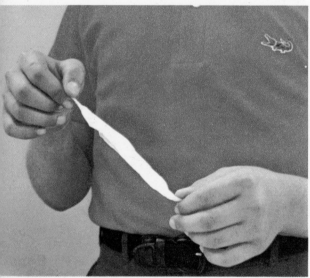

To get an idea of what can happen when fuel and an "oxidizer" combine, try this experiment outdoors:

First, get a bottle, a cork, some vinegar, baking soda (bicarbonate of soda), tissue paper, vaseline, a spoon, and several round pencils.

Put some vaseline where the bottle and cork will touch.

Then, half fill the bottle with a mixture of 50 per cent water and 50 per cent vinegar. (This is the "fuel.")

Put two teaspoonfuls of baking soda (the "oxidizer") in a piece of tissue paper and twist the ends.

Slip the baking soda into the bottle; and, before the paper can come loose and release the baking soda, cork the bottle and place it across several of the pencils.

When the paper comes apart and the baking soda combines with the vinegar, a strong chemical reaction takes place which releases a large quantity of fast-moving, expanding gases.

In a moment . . .

the cork and part of the contents are shot from the bottle, perhaps as far as 20 feet. As a reaction, the bottle has been pushed in the opposite direction.

Incidentally, toy flying rockets usually use chemicals similar to vinegar and baking soda.

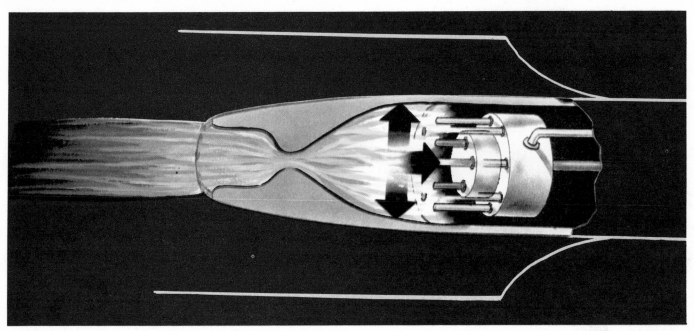

In an actual rocket, fuel and liquid oxygen burn fiercely when they combine. The combustion heats and greatly expands these liquids so that, like water turning to steam, they become gas. The expansion takes place very rapidly and builds fantastic pressure.

Since there is a nozzle at the rear, the rocket shoots ahead.

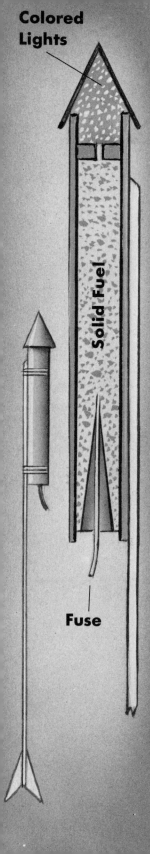

Colored Lights

Solid Fuel

Fuse

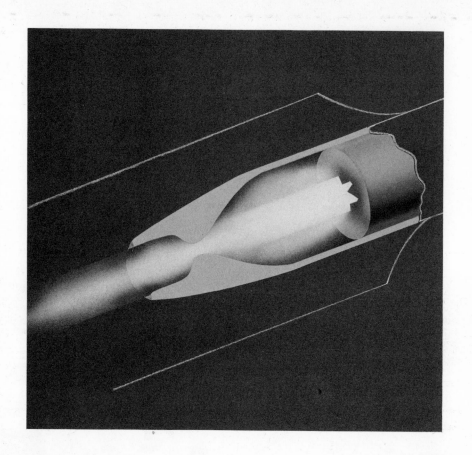

Some rockets use solid instead of liquid fuel. Solid fuel does not require two separate tanks. Instead, the fuel and an oxidizer are mixed together into a plastic, then hardened. This solid fuel is placed right inside the engine.

A Fourth of July skyrocket is an example of a solid-fuel rocket.

These devices were first used by the Chinese nearly a thousand years ago.

Many unmanned rockets have already been shot into outer space, but we have only begun to build rocket ships that will carry people . . . and these will not go far beyond the earth. These early craft, like the one shown here, look much like jet planes. They do not, of course, have air intakes; since the engines don't use air. But they do have wings to assist them when re-entering the earth's heavy atmosphere.

Within your lifetime, scientists and engineers expect to make rockets which will carry us to other worlds. These ships will probably come in several sections, or stages, with the early stages dropping away when their fuel is used up. To "break away" from the earth's gravity, the final stage will have to travel more than 24,000 miles an hour!

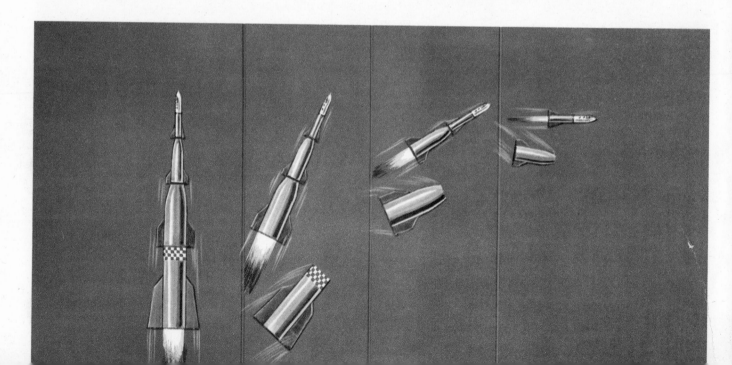

Do you think you'll one day be in a ship like this, on your way to the moon?

Index

9 6 8   F.W.